BRIAN J. POMBO

9 Ways to Amazon-Proof Your Business

How to STAND OUT in Your Industry & Make Every Competitor Irrelevant

First published by BrianJPombo 2020

First edition

ISBN: 978-1-64921-401-0

This book was professionally typeset on Reedsy.
Find out more at reedsy.com

Contents

Preface

Why would you want to be Amazon-Proof?

Amazon.com, Inc. was founded in 1994 under the name Cadabra, Inc. Since that time, they have risen up and raked in over $200 billion in annual revenue, and they have taken over the field of online shopping.

Originally eCommerce meant selling *electronically* through your website on the World Wide Web. People would find you via your URL, an Internet address typed into a browser, or via a search engine when they only knew *what* they were looking for,the generic name for the product or service, but not *who*,your specific brand name.

Today, when someone knows *what* they are looking for, they will most often start out searching in two places:

#1. Amazon.com. So many people have their app installed on their phone and will go directly there.

#2. Google.com. When using this search engine to find products, Amazon is usually among the first results shown.

If you sell products that are also sold on Amazon.com, you are left with only a few options:

#1. Partner WITH Amazon. Sell your products via Amazon

and give them a huge cut of the revenue.

#2. Compete WITH Amazon. Build your company to $200 billion plus in revenue and build a reputation that will garner the attention of Google.

Partnering with Amazon may work with certain products. Some larger companies MAY be able to compete directly with Amazon, due to their position in the marketplace.

Let's face the facts: Neither of these options are optimal long-term. So, what other options are there?

The best way to beat Amazon, is neither to join nor to compete directly with them. The best way to defeat Amazon is to do the things they can not or will not do.

Amazon.com currently runs the eCommerce game due their fast service and cheap prices. So, where can YOU win?

Whether Amazon.com is competition for your business or not, the ***9 Ways to Amazon-Proof Your Business*** that I uncover here will make you impervious to ANY competitive force for the entire lifetime of your business. Keep reading.

But First, A Personal Confession:

This is my first book. At the moment I'm writing these words, I have not published any other book though I certainly plan to.

It's important that I'm honest with you about how it was

produced, because you may otherwise find out on your own. The original outline of these chapters and many of the words within, did not originate from my typing fingers. Neither did they enter the world from the end of a pen onto paper.

Dear Reader, these words were spoken and broadcast live over the Internet through my daily "Brian J. Pombo Live" program. Following it's disbursement, I had it transcribed. I then rearranged some items, and enhanced the content. I edited and proofread it and had others edit and proofread it some more. Finally, I prepared it for publishing.

I always look for the quickest, yet cleanest, way to get my goals accomplished. Hopefully, my ease in producing this content will not take away any of your enjoyment in consuming it.

Please let me know what you think.

Go to: brianjpombo.com/amazonbookreview

Leave me an honest assessment. As this is my first time, please be firm, but gentle, in your critique.

Thank you so much for purchasing. I cannot wait to see what you do with these strategies.

Acknowledgement

There are way too many people that lead me to writing this book. Instead of an exhaustive list, I'm going to focus on thanking and acknowledging these humans:

First, my wife Kate and children Tyler, Alexandra, and Lucas. Without them, I would have put off writing a book for an additional ten to twenty years. With them, anything is possible.

Second, my business partner in crime, marketing genius, and all around great guy Sean E. Douglas. Without whom, there just would never be a book. It would never get done. Ever.

And finally, a very special thanks to:

- Angie Zambrano pro_ebookcovers for an amazing cover design, and
- Michele L. Mathews at Beach Girl Publishing for a fabulous editing job.

1

1st Way: Determine Focus

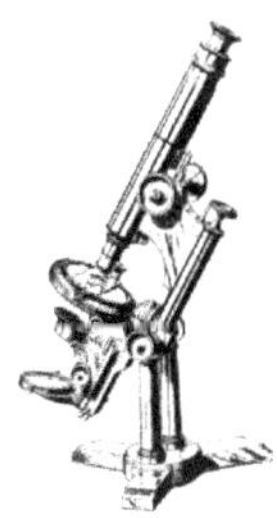

You may be thinking, "Well, the type of products we provide are special. We don't compete with Amazon."

As I mentioned, you probably compete with somebody, whether it's Jeff Bezos over at Amazon, or whether it's somebody else, Amazon is a good foil for us to use.

A lot of people see Jeff as the devil and I don't know whether he is or if he's just an alien overlord that's here to study us as a species.

I *can* tell you one thing: Amazon is moving things.

They're moving the way things are done online, whether you like it or not. So, there's a lot of things that they're doing that are completely changing how we all handle business.

First is commoditization. Amazon is able to take a certain number of products and completely commoditize them. They're able to make everything look the same.

When you think about commodities, you may think of meat or corn or other raw products that are on the commodity market. They all have one price.

What's the difference between one guy's beef and another guy's beef that they're selling? There's probably a lot of differences in quality. There's a lot of different characteristics, but for some reason they've been able to commoditize certain items and put them all into one package and say, "this is the price for this" and "this is the going price for that."

That's what a commodity is: when you're able to lump everything together and be able to label it under one category. It's an illusion, but it's a reality of the world we live in.

Notice how easy it is for people to get stuck in this paradigm? Amazon retains control of the marketplace by keeping one branded item (regardless of how many different companies or individuals are selling it) all under the same ad, on the same page. They've been able to commoditize nearly their entire website.

How do competing retailers differentiate their product from the other seemingly identical ones?

You can't highlight customer service. You can't bundle it together with other items that you know would go well together. You can't even communicate with the customer beyond the ways Amazon allows.

The only option they allow you to differentiate is on price. There's only one direction you can take that price, and that's down. Lower and lower and lower.

This in turn leads the customer the wrong direction. It distorts their vision away from caring about quality, service, and relationship with the seller to, "I'm just looking for the cheapest one." Amazon, by design, forces people to look for the cheapest - and nothing else.

This is how Amazon has painted themselves into a corner. They've trained the sellers to provide the cheapest price and buyers to chase the cheapest price. The price has become the only determinant.

If you've been a slave to this system, it messes with your head, because you think you have to run our businesses that way. You have to make sure you're the cheapest, even when competing with Amazon on your own website.

On top of that, in the long run this strategy creates disloyalty to brands. What reason do people have to be loyal to *your* product? They won't, because they're fixated on price. Even Amazon's search engine is built so that shoppers can organize all their results by price. What real chance do you have of surviving if you aren't the cheapest guy in town?

Walmart played the same game before Amazon. K-Mart did the same before them. Eventually, a cheaper dealer kills off, or severely damages the last *King of Bargains*. "Long live the king."

There's always someone pushing people into trying to play the cheap game. Stop playing that game!

In addition to commoditizing the world, Amazon is now known as "**The Everything Store**." They provide EVERYTHING! Can you think of many items you can't buy on Amazon?

This perception that they've created (in the minds of most people) has set up EVERYONE to be their customer. With Amazon Prime becoming so common, and distribution centers in or near most cities, they have <u>created shipping expectations that are nearly impossible to compete with</u>.

One time I was talking to the owner of a very large, very famous marine survival and safety supply company. He was the founder. They had been doing mail order for years and they also are now doing very good business online as well.

He was telling me about this "slavery" they now have to the now in-demand concept of "free shipping."

The last time I looked, they're offering free shipping for orders over a hundred dollars, or something like that.

That's a common approach, as it's about the closest a lot of other e-commerce outlets can do as when compared to Amazon's free shipping.

The average website can't offer straight out free shipping. They can't offer it and they certainly can't offer it as fast as Amazon can to the continental 48 states.

It's very difficult to compete with what they are providing. They're getting people's minds to think things. People subconsciously think, "When I order from a website it has got to be fast and shipping has got to be free."

And so a lot of companies, lots of ECOMMERCE OWNERS, have tried to live up to these expectations.

Instead of *changing the expectations* of their customers, they're having to race to catch up... and it depends on their customer market on whether that's a good idea or not.

Amazon has been forcing everyone's minds to shift. Their customers' minds and therefore the minds of business owners and executives (both competitors and partners).

This is why you HAVE TO overcome this mindset.

We all know Amazon's not the only force to be reckoned with. There's many other things that are happening in your industry to contend with. I'm sure that your competition is forcing expectations on you, especially if you aren't the big person on the block.

You've got to be able to break out of that box of expectations. That's what becoming "Amazon Proof" is all about.

The first way to Amazon-Proof is to **DETERMINE FOCUS.**

You have to determine the focus of your company. Determine where you are going. Determine the focus of your time and effort, especially in terms of marketing.

It really all goes back to Jay Abraham's "Three Ways to Grow Any Business."

I'm going to outline them the same way that Russell Brunson, founder of ClickFunnels, does it. He calls them, "Acquisition, Ascension and Monetization. "

First, Acquisition means you increase the number of customers. The whole process from taking a person from being a prospect to being a customer.

Next, Ascension is increasing the average transaction price. That's just getting as many clients to pay more for each purchase.

Monetization is increasing the frequency your average customer buys from you.

That's Acquisition, Ascension and Monetization.

No major ideas. Here the thing, though: over and over again, companies focus on only on Acquisition. It is their number one thing, but the easiest way to expand is in Ascension and Monetization.

If you're focused on getting the next customer, and then the next customer, and all the while you're not focused enough (or at all) on your current or past customers, then you are making your job tougher than it needs to be.

If you focused even half of your energy to keeping customers coming back, to building ways for them to do more business with you, your profits can compound.

Knowing these three modes, determine the focus of your company. Determine the focus of the people that you have on staff and to make sure that they know what their job is. If they need be focused beyond just "getting new customers", make sure they know that.

We need to be out to keep the customers we have, make them happier, make sure they have a remarkable experience. And that's what acquisition, ascension, and monetization are all about.

Determine that focus for yourself and your company and you will take a huge step to defeating all your competition because it's the type of things they're not even thinking about.

Get Focused Now!
Sign up for the "Get Focused Now Strategy Session"
Go to BrianJPombo.com/focus/

2

2nd Way: Be Consistent

How would you like to kill your competition? Just completely wipe them out.

I'm not talking about hurting anybody, but what if you could actually do away with all the businesses that are getting in your way of dominating your marketplace?

This is what **Amazon Proofing** your business is all about. It means making your business completely competition-proof - from top to bottom, even against someone as big as Amazon.com.

This step might seem boring, but I'm dedicating a chapter to it because I have not yet found a way around it. Trust me - if I could find a way around this step, I would. This is the least exciting or colorful concept in the book, which should also be a clue as to how important it is.

This is step is deceptively simple, but it is so essential, and it's not one of those that come naturally to most.

The number two way is, **BE CONSISTENT**.

Be consistent in everything you're doing to reach your potential, your past and your current customers. You have to be consistent, because so few are.

Anyone that has become really good at any form of marketing, in any one area, has had to be consistent with it.

You may normally think of marketing as only being targeted towards people that don't know anything about you yet. Maybe, to try and bring them in and make them new customers.

It's more than that.

I mentioned Russell Brunson briefly in the last chapter, and I discuss him and his concepts a lot on my daily videos. At one time, Russell got really good at being consistent at doing webinars. He did them every week for years on end. Live webinars. He did them consistently just long enough to really understand that medium and to be able to take advantage of it on many levels. For years, he has taught others his method that he calls, "The Perfect Webinar."

Ben Settle, (another expert I mention on my videos and podcast), is another example of this. He is really well known as THE email go-to-guy. He is known as a major expert at email marketing.

How does he do it?

Simple. He send emails out daily.

That's right, every single day Ben sends an email out to the people that opt-in to his email list. It was tough for me to imagine dealing with an email every single day from someone, but if you're a good enough writer, you can pull it off. After I joined his list, I saw what was possible. Ben truly is a master of his craft.

How do you become a good enough writer to write an email every day AND keep in interesting?

You guessed right: you've got to be consistent. It's all about sticking with something (ANY method of communication) long enough to get good at it and to really understand how to use it properly to reach people.

I tend to bring up various principles brought up by others. What I've found over the years is that the best principles tend to be true throughout the generations. That is to say, while I may hear it from one person the first time... it's no surprise when I stumble upon the same principle being talked about from past experts in regards to different situations.

On occasion, I hear someone say the same principal in a much simpler, easier to understand way, than I originally heard or read it. One person who has a knack for simplifying principles is a guy named Dean Jackson.

One thing Dean talks about is the concept of the "*Before*, *During* and *After Units*" in regards to your business. This is a great idea to use when planning out your consistent marketing strategy.

These "Units" are really useful for understanding the relationship you have with your customers and clients during the entire business cycle.

Any eventual customer starts out as a "prospective customers." Then they go through a period when they are an active customer. With most, they eventually stop using your products and services. That's the cycle.

Divide up everything you do in your Marketing into "Before", "During" and "After." It helps to clarify everything.

The "*Before Unit*" is outreach. It's job is to bring people in. Getting people to "**Know, Like and Trust you**."

> ***"All things being equal people will do business with, and refer business to, those people they know, like, and trust."***

– The Go-Giver *by Bob Burg and John David Mann*

Those who buy in are brought into the "*During Unit*," the time in which you deliver your goods and services to them.

Finally the "*After Unit*," is when you communicate with former customers to try and bring them back into the During Unit. That's the whole idea: get the right people back to the During Unit, because that's where the money making relationship happens.

What's this have to do with consistency?

How consistent are you in marketing to any of these places, let alone all three?

Oftentimes, we only focus on the Before Unit, and put very little focus on the During and After Units. We just don't put as much focus on people we're already working with. We take them for granted.

We especially ignore people after they leave us and enter into the After Unit. Few businesspeople do ANYTHING to try and win them back. Are you ignoring this goldmine?

Why not find out why they left? Offer them something to get them back through the doorway. Once you find something that works, consistently deliver that message to others who enter the After Unit.

What are you doing at each Unit? Have you ever gotten a new customer, retained current ones, or brought old ones "back to life"? Have you created ongoing systems to consistently repeat that action?

Get with your team or sit down on your own. Write up a plan for each phase in the business cycle. Implement it. Stick to it. Do it long enough to where you know whether it's profitable for you or not.

That's a huge piece to developing consistency that I've found.

Any owner or executive can sit down and find out whether your company is actually properly paying attention to each of those areas or not. You can find out whether you're being consistent in each of those areas.

Do it. Hold yourself to it. Or hire someone to watch over it.

Keep Consistent Forever!
Sign up for the "Consistent Systems Strategy Session"
Go to BrianJPombo.com/consistency/

3

3rd Way: Be Different

If you're looking to completely demolish your competition, you are in the right place, keep reading. We're on our way.

This third step is so cliche', so commonly discussed, you may just think I'm wasting your time. "This guy can't possibly be real."

I am. This step is, also, not negotiable.

The number three step to Amazon Proofing your business is **BE**

DIFFERENT.

Be Different.

Now what do I mean by "be different?" I know - It's so broad. It's tough to even wrap your mind around what being different means, especially if you have already committed to the other steps.

Even if you're in direct competition with Amazon.com, you're going to want to focus on being different. Not just different from them, different from EVERYBODY else in your industry.

I am not saying to go out there and be something you're not, but be different. Find a different message or find a new way to deliver the same message. Find a different media format to reach your audience and marketplace. Be Different.

The most difficult thing for most people is creativity. Oftentimes, the most creative person at the company is you (the owner or the decision-maker). I know when you first started, creativity escaped from every pore as you developed the business from a small seed of an idea to what it is today.

Eventually in the course of most businesses, it becomes very difficult to be creative because you get bogged down in all the details of the business and it takes you away from what your really most natural at, which is the creative side of things.

You created the business, especially if you're the founder. You're probably creating all the time, BUT are you making things different?

Here's a couple of places that I look for inspiration in my company, as well as helping other business owners in their company:

The first is a book by marketer Bill Glazer called "Outrageous Advertising That's Outrageously Successful." This whole book is nothing but examples of advertising that he used for his menswear store. It is filled with stories of outrageous advertising examples he tried in his business over the years. He got really good at reaching people with different methods: through the mail, the radio, the newspaper, the TV.

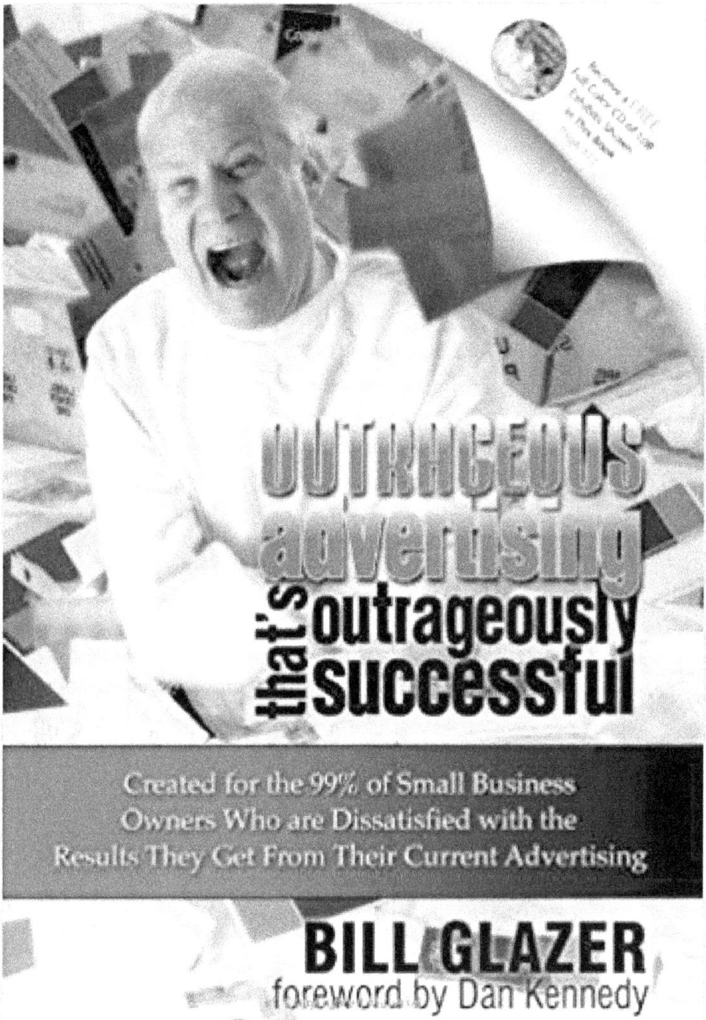

The cover of the book shows a great example, Bill screaming in a straight jacket. That is a photo, advertising or not, that demands attention. Bill was really good at finding different wacky costumes and situations that would make his advertising

STAND OUT. Have you ever seen a store that sells men's suits advertise like that?

Bill really used the *Number Four* way of Amazon Proofing yourself, which is to **Be Somebody** (you'll see in the next chapter).

Bill put himself out there! He's not all that outgoing of a person, either, but he knew that his store needed a personality that people could recognize and connect to. So, Bill became that personality for his business. Even though his business was started by his father, he put himself out there as the personality. and that's a really big deal.

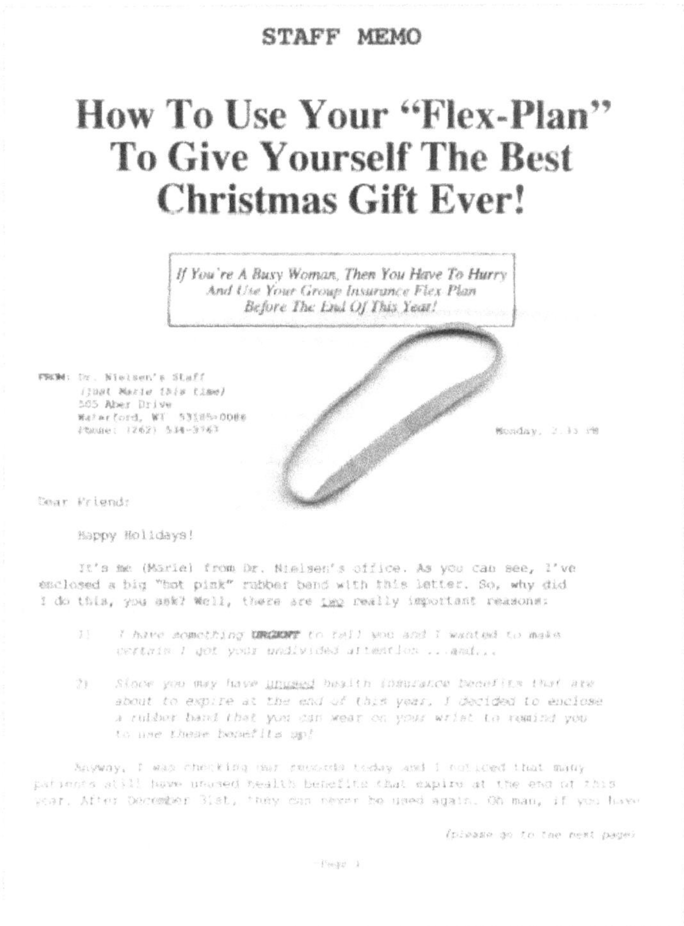

STAFF MEMO

How To Use Your "Flex-Plan" To Give Yourself The Best Christmas Gift Ever!

If You're A Busy Woman, Then You Have To Hurry And Use Your Group Insurance Flex Plan Before The End Of This Year!

FROM: Dr. Nielsen's Staff
(Just Marie this time)
565 Aber Drive
Waterford, WI 53185-0088
Phone: (262) 534-3763

Monday, [illegible]

Dear Friend:

Happy Holidays!

It's me (Marie) from Dr. Nielsen's office. As you can see, I've enclosed a big "hot pink" rubber band with this letter. So, why did I do this, you ask? Well, there are two really important reasons:

1) *I have something* **URGENT** *to tell you and I wanted to make certain I got your undivided attention ...and...*

2) *Since you may have unused health insurance benefits that are about to expire at the end of this year, I decided to enclose a rubber band that you can wear on your wrist to remind you to use these benefits up!*

Anyway, I was checking our records today and I noticed that many patients still have unused health benefits that expire at the end of this year. After December 31st, they can never be used again. Oh man, if you have

(please go to the next page)

-Page 1-

This is a mailer (from page 123) that he sent out to people that had **already been to his store**. Inside it had an actual rubber band. In direct-response styled mail, they call that a "grabber" or "lumpy mail" because when you fold up the letter in the envelope, something that isn't quite flat sticks out. In feeling the envelope, many will open it just to find out what's inside.

If you know anything about advertising via direct mail, getting people to open and look at it is much of the battle.

Imagine, having an ongoing campaign to people you've already had as customers before.

Bill's book is filled with a whole bunch of wacky stuff like that. No need to copy his ideas directly, but let them inspire you to think differently.

Remember, ANYTHING you do publicly for your business is marketing and advertising. You don't even have to use the same mediums. Just take these concepts and be different in front of your audience.

Another book I use to spark creative juices is called, *Steal Like An Artist,* by Austin Kleon.

I reviewed Austin's other book Show Your Work a couple of years back on my YouTube channel.

The whole concept of *Steal Like An Artist* is that you can be creative without feeling like you have to dredge something out of the ether and be completely original.

You can be different just by combining a couple other things together. Austin uses example after example of how all artists do this - all artists out there are taking what they've experienced in life and from other artists, and all they do is they combine this with that, and THAT creates something "new."

To a degree, even The Beatles didn't create anything new. They took different styles of music, combined them together and created something that was unusual. Sure, it was a little bit different than what people were used to. Yet they delivered it in a way that was just familiar enough to take the entire popular music of the day in a new direction.

Austin uses example after example of that in this book. It's a really simple book - nothing but big print and pictures, really. Still, the concept is so strong, that it gets the point across. It's one of those books I go back to again and again. If I feel stuck somewhere, I'll go back and just flip through it, find something random, and read a few lines. It gets me right back in the swing of things.

It also helps you to take other things in your life, things you enjoy, how to be able to take those, meld them in to what you're doing with your business.

You have got to be different. You have got to stand out and be a little bit outrageous, a little bit daring. Do that and... **you're going to go far beyond your competition because you don't see Amazon.com out there being outrageous and crazy - nor the majority of your competition in your field - if anyone at all!**

Every once in awhile, you see a big company doing it right for a short period of time and they'll get attention. For some reason they never stick with it, but those are the times when they get the most momentum.

If you're willing to do it (or have someone on your team do it), it will make you stand out from the crowd of competitors that your customer base is already aware of. There's always a way to be different from the people, company or products that you're competing against.

What Makes You Different?

Sign up for the "Difference Maker Strategy Session"

Go to BrianJPombo.com/differencemaker/

4

4th Way: Be Somebody

Do you suffer from indigestion? Maybe huge amounts of stomach acid or possibly ulcers. And can you link any of those symptoms back to the stress you have regarding your business - regarding the competition that you're up against?

It may even be someone as big as Amazon.com.

Keep going, we don't want you dying before you've had a chance to at least review all these steps and get them implemented in your business.

The number four way to Amazon-Proof in your business has a lot to do with this little scene here. This is from the movie "The Jerk", starring Steve Martin. Awesome movie. It's very corny, very goofy, but it has a whole lot of truths in it.

And one of the big truths is, I think, signified by this picture right here. In the story, our protagonist Navin (played by Steve Martin) has had a drink put together - in just the right way - to copy this specific ad he saw. The top of the ad it says, "Be Somebody."

When it comes to making a huge change, and defeating the big guys, you need to have yourself or someone else in your business be someone.

The number four way to Amazon-Proof your business is to **BE SOMEBODY.**

Somebody has to be the *spokesperson*, be a *celebrity*, or maybe even the *expert.* You need a person like that on your team. If you're anything like me, it might be a little difficult to step out and say, "Hey, I'm the person and I want to use this whole interaction we're having."

Here's an example:

Last year I decided to switch my company over, move everything over to center around my name because it's a centerpiece to tie in to what I'm working on going forward.

We changed everything over to "BrianJPombo.com", my entire company's name is "BrianJPombo.com LLC." Everything is directing back to that center source.

This is not because I like promoting myself. I really don't.

I do like being the center of attention. Don't get me wrong, but I don't like promoting my name or myself or setting myself up as any type of expert.

At the same time, I do have a certain expertise in the areas of helping people to be able to take their business from where it is to where they want to be. That's what I'm all about, showing others how to really transform their business into their DREAM BUSINESS.

But I digress. If you're looking to really take things and make your company competition proof... you've got to make it about you. You've got to be someone.

If you're looking at tackling this alone, here are a couple recommendations for further research:

The book *Expert Secrets*, by Russell Brunson. It's all about this topic. How do you convince others that you should be trusted? This is a great book for that.

Also, *Celebrity Branding YOU.* I actually met Nick Nanton (one of the collaborators on this book) a few years back in Orlando when I was at a Glazer-Kennedy Inner Circle event. He's a really sharp guy. He's won Emmys for his film work. He's currently involved with Operation Underground Railroad. He just produced a great film for them.

This book is actually a pretty good. I mean "celebrity branding" is their terminology. The whole idea is to become a celebrity expert in your field regardless of what business you have.

Any business has the ability to create a "someone" in it.

It's really helpful to have someone out front that people can relate with. They don't have to think you're great. They don't have to think you're horrible. They just have to relate with you as a person, even if your personality doesn't match them.

Your audience is more likely going to listen to what you have to say and it all comes back to those three things. Know, Like and Trust.

I know it's corny, but they have to know who you are. They have to like you to some extent, and they have to be able to trust you. Having yourself as "someone" allows that process to occur. They eventually know who you are and then they start to get to like you and eventually they trust you. That's what number four is all about.

What Makes You Different?

Sign up for the "Celebrity Creation Strategy Session"

Go to BrianJPombo.com/celebrity/

5

5th Way: Offer Belonging

Who is your main competition? Is it Amazon.com? Is it somebody else? Regardless of who it is, it doesn't matter how big they are or what they have over on you. You *can* do things they can't.

Out of the top 9 ways to Amazon-Proof your business, let's go over Number Five. Number Five is a very, very interesting one and deals with a little bit of dark magic.

Number five way to overcome competition is what I call **OFFER BELONGING**.

If you can offer your ideal audience a sense of belonging, you're going to see something occur that most companies can never truly develop - and there's a reason why: They never even tried to develop it.

This step is really about focusing on developing culture. Oftentimes when you hear people talking about developing culture, they're talking about inside the company. They're talking about all your employees, vendors, and so forth.

I was just on Linkedin.com, earlier today. I saw Gary Vaynerchuk talking about it, and then I saw another lady talking about it and they were talking about culture on the exact day that I wanted to bring up culture. So I listened into what they were about and they're talking about culture within the company, and that's great. It's something really important to think and talk about, but it's something different than what I'm suggesting.

If you want to overcome competition, especially if they are the big guys in your industry, (even if it's Amazon.com), the one thing they have a difficult time producing is culture within their **customer community**.

Giant companies (and I know "giant" is a relative term) are spread too thin. They have too many different types of people as customers. They're trying to appeal to everyone. They have more than a "difficult time" creating that sense of belonging. The task is nearly impossible for them.

You, on the other hand, with the right desire and focus, should be able to produce belonging in your market.

Especially if you're business plays to a niche area. If you're into beekeeping, if you're into soap making, if you're into a survival tools, these are very niche areas. These are the types of people that have a tough time finding like-minded people like themselves.

I want to mention the book *Expert Secrets* by Russell Brunson. This is a really good book that deals with this idea.

In *Expert Secrets*, Russell talks about the three things you need to really create a mass movement. If you're looking to take your business to the next level, this is a great thing to focus on.

Number one: Each mass movement has a charismatic leader or attractive character. No matter who these leaders are (good, evil or otherwise); whether they are Adolf Hitler or Jesus Christ, they all display similar patterns.

Number two: Each movement had a message that was focused on a future-based cause that is bigger than themselves.

Number three: They each offered their audience a new "opportunity" versus a mere "improvement."

I really want to focus on **Number two**, because that "future-based cause" is one thing that can unite everybody in terms of having a real culture that can be latched on to. Especially if you have a cause that's bigger than each of their individual issues.

An example of this is Beepods.com. Beepods is headed up by Brad James. Go and listen to the Off-the-Grid Biz Podcast episode where I interviewed Brad. In it, he goes through their cause and about their focus on fixing the colony collapse issues. That's the disappearing honey bees problem that has been talked about for a number of years.

Colony collapse is a huge focus on what they're doing and they're collecting data from everybody that uses their hive system in order to be able to find out what's actually causing the disappearance of bees as well as what isn't. There are a lot of myths out there, and Brad is interested in uncovering the facts.

He also discusses how adopting that cause has allowed them to grow as a company and gain attention they would not have otherwise attained.

Having a cause really creates *a feeling* more than anything else. There's got to be a feeling that a person gets by being around your products and by being around your group of customers. If your customers have the ability to belong and are able to meet together and connect - that's a great feeling to impart.

A really big part of that process ties into Chapter Six, where we will be discussing the offering ongoing subscriptions. Subscriptions can take the form of a membership or a club. That club can become a product unto itself. The community you build can become a product in its own right.

You can not beat the uniqueness of a community. Like I mentioned, that Beepods episode really focuses on that aspect of business.

Here's another book, this one is called *The True Believer*, by Eric Hoffer. This is one scary book. This isn't something I recommend that everyone run out and get, but if you're interested in creating a culture, or creating a sense of belonging, it's very detailed. This is an interesting piece that goes into the human nature (good and bad) behind groups.

It's an older book, in comparison to the others I recommend here. It was first published in 1951, and specifically it is all about mass movements. It's very similar to what Russell Brunson was talking about: what causes people to join or flee from any form of mass movement.

It's a smaller book, but very dense writing. Like I said, this isn't for everybody, but if you want to get into the psychology behind groups, *The True Believer* is a fascinating read.

Build Belonging Into Your Business!
Sign up for the "Belonging Builder Strategy Session"
Go to BrianJPombo.com/belonging/

6

6th Way: Offer Ongoing

Next, let's get into the concept of *timing*. The timing in which you do one action or another in your business is imperative to whether you achieve your goal desired result. Timing is the difference between success and failure.

Before we get into that and go deeper into the subject, I want to discuss what's been happening today and it has to do with the unpredictability of business itself.

So, at this time, I'm supposed to be at a housewarming party for my friends Jered and Jessica. They just bought a new house.

I wish I could have made it, but I got behind while working on business. Sorry, I'm not there.

I really have had a crazy day and ended up in a bunch of places I wasn't expecting to. While at home, I bent down to pick something up while he cabinet was open, and hit my head right into it. So, if you could see me, you'd notice a great big knot on my forehead.

Things just don't always happen as they're planned. You know what I'm saying? It's just one of those days and it's something to remember when dealing with your customers and prospects.

Everyone has a LOT going on in their lives. The moment you connect with them through and advertisement or other communication may just not be the right moment to catch their attention. This is where your timing matters most.

One of the most common things I come across, especially new clients, is that there are always inconsistencies present in their business. I'll give you an example regarding one of my clients:

Phil (not his real name) had one long period of great sales coming through his website. Year after year and month after month he didn't have to do too much work to keep the profits rolling in.

Then came a downturn in his business. It was at that point he asked for my help. In his defense, the changes were due to the overall economy and not due to any direct changes he made to the business.

The way it worked was that his main source of revenue came from selling books and DVDs, as well as other media items in his niche. As those sales slumped, he was looking for something more consistent.

What I advised him to do is a deceptively simple concept, but it's beyond most people that run websites or run businesses online. Most managers of ecommerce stores have a very difficult time applying it back to their business.

This concept is the sixth way to Amazon-Proof your business. It's called **OFFER ONGOING**.

The most basic way to think about this are "subscriptions." In other words, get someone to pay on an ongoing basis. This goes back to the Monetization step we covered in Chapter 1.

To truly "monetize" you must get people to purchase more often. **Get them on a subscription, so they're purchasing ongoing without any thought put into it.** Once they subscribe, it continues going on from that point forward.

You may say to yourself, "well...that's an oversimplification of the whole process".

It really isn't. You've got to get the simplicity of it first and then understand all the benefits of it. Here's what I'm going to recommend to you. It's another book you should check out and read: *Automatic Customer, Creating a Subscription Business in Any Industry* by John Warrillow. This is a very, very, very good book.

I've actually given these away to my clients because it is such a powerful book. Especially if you have a tough time thinking about how to apply the subscription model to your business.

So, let's go back to my friend Phil. He had his regular buyers buying books and movies randomly every month or so. What I had him do is set up a "Book of the Month Club" and then eventually a "Movie of the Month Club" and sell the exact same things he was already selling.

See, he had people that would come back every couple of months, get a big stack of books and go away, and then come back again and get some more. People were acting like they were subscribed. We just made it simple for them and automated the process.

Find what people are already buying, put it into a subscription. It's a very simple model. If you're already selling things, it's an extremely simple thing to do.

It's not a game-changing idea unto itself, but Phil had never thought of actually applying it to the books he sold. It was clear though, he had more than enough new and old books for sale on his website that it made sense to offer them as an ongoing subscription.

Subscriptions just make sense. You can apply them to any industry. It really is a huge deal that creates **STABILITY** and **PREDICTABILITY** into your business.

If you make it available and promote it properly to the right people, it can work. Find out what they want first and then deliver it to them (even if it's a digital product) on an ongoing basis. You're going to create revenue predictability and really take away the headaches of your business. Its a simple, simple, simple idea.

Look at what Amazon did with "Amazon Prime." Customers pay on a monthly or annual basis to be a part of Prime. With that payment you get special discounts, free and expedited shipping, as well as a whole bunch of other things including, free streaming tv shows and movies (even some exclusively for Prime members).

If you look at the statistics of what they've been able to do through the years, Amazon customers who subscribe to Prime **purchase <u>more</u> because they're part of the membership**.

They just pile in all these products and services that don't take anything extra for Amazon to be able to provide.

Across the board, people purchase more as soon as they get on Amazon Prime. It's almost an absolute rule that if you're on Prime, you're going to purchase from Amazon more often.

Costco did this, (in a non-digital way), when they introduced their members-only retail shopping model. People that have a membership to go to Costco, go more often than they would have otherwise. Well, of course, they can't go at all if you don't have the membership, but they are encouraged to choose Costco more and more (over competitors) to take advantage of the fact that they're paying annually for that membership.

They want to take advantage of it. There's a good ***feeling*** that goes along with that.

The subscription/membership concept also ties in directly to the Number Five Way, "Offer Belonging." How difficult is it for a person to feel like they belong when they are "Members?"

How else can you "Offer Belonging" while "Offering Ongoing?"

When someone's a member, you've allowed them to buy YOUR attention. If they have a bad day and bump their head, like I did, they'll still be there tomorrow.

Offering Ongoing, means they are invested... in you.

Subscribify Your Business!
Sign up for the "Subscribify Strategy Session"
Go to BrianJPombo.com/subscribify/

7

7th Way: Offer Bigger

If you're ready for this, the Number Seven way, is probably the most deceptively simple concept. This alone, done right, could make a huge change in your business.

This one step, I've taken and used with most of my clients and it always has success. Now you know, in business, there are no guarantees; but I am saying that in my experience, I have been able to achieve success by doing this one thing.

The Number Seven Way is **OFFER BIGGER**.

Remember *Ascension*, that concept we talked about in Chapter 1? Ascension is all about getting customers to spend more per transaction. It's all about raising the dollar amount (or whatever currency you use in your country), raising it higher. Get them to spend more.

There's a whole lot of reasons why you want to do this for the long-term health of your business. One reason is positioning.

There is only **one** lowest-price company in any industry. This plays specifically to the *Amazon* dilemma, because Amazon is the low-price leader in many industries and across many product lines. Like Walmart before them, who has played the low-price game in the physical world. Before Walmart, K-mart was playing the low-price game.

Keep in mind, there's always somebody playing the low price game and there's only one of them that's going to win at being the lowest. It's usually the biggest one because they can afford to take the hit in the short-run. Then, in the long-run, they make money with long-term customer loyalty.

This is a big piece of what Amazon's play has been. Even Jeff Bezos has said, what will likely end Amazon is when someone can come about and either offer higher quality or the same things at a lower price. When Amazon can't afford to compete, they will cease to be the "low-price leader." It's basically, an inevitability.

So, do you *really* want to go head to head with Amazon on that? Are you ready to make or break your business on a race to the bottom?

Let's look at another option:

Let's say you're able to raise your prices, to a point that you can offer higher quality or greater variety or more convenience than most of your competition.

What if you could offer something unique - something that nobody else is offering? What if you take your highest priced item and combine something else with it? Perhaps, you could bring in another item and join them together; or bundle a service along with it?

Value is relative. Find a way to add value then raise the price. Raise the price significantly and you'll be amazed with the result.

There's a whole bunch of ideas. It's endless, really. Start asking yourself these questions and you'll go on forever creating all the different reasons you would want to go about doing this.

Here's some background on the psychology. There was this study done by the University of Bonn, in Germany. (Go and check it out: https://www.uni-bonn.de/news/189-2017)

They did a blind study on participants and had everybody in MRI scanners. They had tubes going in and they were telling them, "okay, we're about to give you a wine that's worth this much money." Then they had them taste it.

"Now, we're about to give you a wine that's worth this much.

Next, try this wine that's worth a whole lot more." They gave them different prices for each wine that they were having them drink. Afterwards, they rated each one.

After each drink, they gave him some neutral liquid, you know, water or whatever to rinse out their mouth and cleanse their palate. Then they'd try the next one and they said, "okay, grade each of these."

Without fail, across the board, each person graded them in accordance to the price that they were given. The catch was, the prices weren't real. In fact, there were only two wines that they gave them throughout the test.

Obviously, this wouldn't work if you had two wines that were extremely different, say, a low quality in comparison to high quality one. It would probably be less likely to work. What they did though, is found one wine that was average and one that was quite a bit better.

They found that no matter which one they were drinking, the participants consciously believe the higher priced wines were of higher quality and taste.

The best part of this study isn't what they said out loud, but what their brains showed behind-the-scenes.

It's not just that the price was messing with their logical side. The pleasure areas in their brain lit up higher when drinking the "higher-priced" wine, and less pleasure was visible for the "lower-priced" ones. They actually, physically enjoyed it more when they believed it cost more.

Here's the dirty little secret: people like spending more money.

Think about the things you like spending more money on. And, I know, there's a lot of us out there that are cheapskates and we don't like spending more money on almost anything; but think about the things you're willing to spend a little bit more money on - every once in awhile.

Aren't those the things you get the most pleasure from? Aren't those of the things you get the most enjoyment over?

It's no accident. There is a direct correlation.

Here's the good news: You can actually help your customers to enjoy your products and services more by raising your prices.

Now, don't get me wrong. I am NOT saying just go out right now and, across the board, raise your prices. That's not that's not necessarily needed.

What I am saying is, you should add some more quality to what you're selling and then raise your prices. Add a little bit extra and then bump the price up. Give a reason for it and have it be real. Make it meaningful.

You go and do that and you just might change your business overnight.

If you are having a cashflow issue with your business, and need an "injection", this is the first thing I recommend. Go through and finding out how you can plus your products and services and then increase your prices.

Even if you only did it with your top-tier items, you may see a difference in behavior from your customers, but you may be surprised how little it affects the amount sold.

Expand Your Business Offerings!
Sign up for the "Business Pump Up Strategy Session"
Go to BrianJPombo.com/bizpumpup/

8

8th Way: Make Offers More Often

All right. Next, we're going to go over Number Eight.

The Number Eight way to Amazon-Proof your business is:

MAKE OFFERS MORE OFTEN.

So, let's pull it back a bit. When you sit down and pay attention to radio commercials you hear, to TV commercials you see, to the commercials you see streaming through YouTube (or wherever you are online); ask yourself how many times they make an actual offer.

What is an offer? How do you define an offer?

An offer is, "if you do this, you'll get that" or "we'll give you that." It is asking the audience to take a specific action in exchange for specific action or thing.

Another way of looking at an *offer*, (as I'm defining it), is the phrase "*Call-To-Action*" or "*CTA*". It's calling for the audience to act.

If you start paying attention to commercial messages, you too will notice that very few advertisers have a specific CTA or offer. Large, well-known brands, with often times the most memorable commercials, are not asking the audience to do anything.

It's not that they completely throwing away their money. What they are doing most often is trying to get you to feel a certain way about a brand. Sometimes they are just trying to tell you the brand name or get the logo out there in front of you, to build long-term familiarity.

This *can work*, but takes a lot of money and time. If you have plenty of both of those, you don't need to be efficient. Anyone who has ever worked for or with a large corporation knows that efficiency is usually not the top priority. Waste abounds, and their advertising is usually not immune.

How do you beat their inefficient and vague advertisements?

You guessed it: make an actual offer! Making offers really helps get things moving. This is how you beat the big guys with their huge names and bloated budgets.

You have to offer something specific, more often.

Here's an example. Nearly every time I do a live video chat or recorded audio podcast, I make an offer. I've only had two where it just slipped my mind to even make the offer. Other than that, every single time, I make the offer. Those of you who watch on a regular basis, you already know what it is.

The first year I focused on promoting "DreamBizChat.com."

I always say something like,

> *"If you are the owner of an executive of a company in the self-reliance space, (meaning that you have a company that helps people to become more self-reliant through your products or services, then I'm going to encourage you to go to DreamBizChat.com. At DreamBizChat.com, you can watch the eight and a half minute video I have there. If you like what I'm talking about, fill out the application for a chance to talk to me. Now, normally I charge $600 and above for people to be able to talk to me and have a strategy session.*
>
> *At the end of our strategy session, you are going to walk away with a plan on what to do with your business; to take it to your dream business level, as you define it.*

> *Whether you want to be able to have more time, more revenue or just have the freedom to do what you want to do, go to DreamBizChat.com and fill out that form."*

You see that's an offer. It's simple.

I'm not asking for any money, but it is an offer. You go and do this, and this is what you're going to get for it.

When I forget to do it, I feel like kicking myself, because it's the main reason I spend time to create these media messages.

If you "offer more often", you're going to *get more often.* This is all based on a principle and you can find this talked about all throughout marketing circles, and direct response marketing specifically.

There's one guy that really explains it well. Read Dan Kennedy's *No B.S. Direct Marketing: The Ultimate No Holds Barred Kick Butt Take No Prisoners Direct Marketing for Non-Direct Marketing*

Businesses. It's a great book. Perfect if you're unfamiliar with direct-response advertising. Don't be fooled by the cartoony cover.

There's some serious lessons in here. One of my favorites is his number one rule, "There will always be an offer or offers."

Whatever you are putting out there into the world, always have an offer attached. What have you got to lose?

If you do that, if you do it more often, it's one more way to put yourself up and over your competition.

Now, adding this step alone is guaranteed to add value to your business, but this works perfectly in conjunction with the eight other ways to be able to Amazon-Proof your business.

Make Sure Your Offer Is Ready!
Sign up for the "Offer Injection Strategy Session"
Go to BrianJPombo.com/offer/

9

9th Way: Be Everywhere

If you do all the other steps, this is the one that's the cherry on top. This is the one that'll make everything else ten times more powerful.

Do you really want to get the applause from your crowd of people you're trying to get attention from?

Next, we are going to cover the Ninth and final way to completely Amazon-Proof your business. Putting all of these ways into effect will keep your business free from all of your current perceived competition. Take them to heart. If you take these and put them fully into motion, you will completely dominate your marketplace and build a loyal following. You will eventually have people cheering for you all over the world.

The 9th, and final way is: **BE EVERYWHERE**.

Be Ubiquitous. Go and look it up. It means be everywhere. Be Everywhere.

You've got to be on everyone's lips. You've got to be everywhere you can.

This doesn't just mean be "everywhere online." You should be "everywhere offline" as well. If there is another option, you should be there too.

It doesn't just mean paid advertising. It doesn't just mean the free stuff, and the organic ranking in search engines. It means everything.

I don't mean do everything. Do everything that you can to be in front of your market. Stay away from actions and advertising that do not produce profitable results. Either something is worth your money, time and life force, or it isn't.

In addition, be willing to pay for every type of advertising that works. Define the end goal of your ads, track results, and MAKE them work for you.

One thing that will help is to pay attention to where your market is.

Where are they hanging out? What are they doing? Are you in front of them all at all times?

Are they driving to work on a certain freeway? Are you on the billboard? Do you have a person waving a sign?

You may say, "I don't have a physical location."

It doesn't matter whether you do or you don't. The details are irrelevant. Try to get this principle. Are you taking advantage of everything you possibly can? Are you, at least, allowing yourself to think about the possibilities?

Obviously, you probably can't even afford ALL the possibilities, but do you have them written down somewhere?

Are the people on your staff thinking about these things? Here's an idea, get them together once regularly and brainstorm every possible way to get yourself out there in front of your ideal customer. You may be surprised about the amazing ideas coming from your least-experienced team members.

That's what "be everywhere" is all about. Being everywhere is a mindset, if you work with a team, it's a culture.

Here's some online examples of people who are currently, purposely "everywhere."

Gary Vaynerchuk. If you watch any form of online business videos, you've certainly seen and heard this guy.

He goes by "Gary Vee" for short. Outrageous, vulgar, and unapologetic - Gary is everywhere.

Grant Cardone. Another controversial "guru." This guy is everywhere.

It doesn't matter whether you like these people or dislike these people, they are everywhere.

You know who they are. More than likely than not, you know

your position on them.

So, who are the people that stand out within your marketplace? Are there any leaders, experts or celebrities that everyone knows? Does anyone represents the gold standard, that anyone else would be compared to? Who are they? Does your company have that type of impact? Do you or someone in your company have that kind of impact?

Being everywhere is not without it's headaches. You, or someone at your company, must be willing to take the arrows that are absolutely coming your way as you become better known. You have to be willing to take a stand. It may mean having a whole portion of the people, possibly, who take a stand against you and your company.

Are you willing to do that? Are you doing that on a regular basis? This is what be everywhere is all about.

Being everywhere truly takes all the other 8 steps, and everything else that you're doing and it magnifies it tenfold, a hundred fold, etc. Get started. Go out there and do it.

Become Omnipresent to Your Customers!
Sign up for the "Omnipresence Strategy Session"
Go to BrianJPombo.com/omnipresence/

10

Wrap Up

Well, hopefully you have discovered as you flipped through these pages that "competition" is a state of mind. You can't lose, if you refuse to play the game.

How does one "refuse to play the game?"

Stand out so far away from the competition in how you run your company, that no one will even bring you up in the same breath. Use these Nine Ways to stand out, and no one, not even Amazon could be considered your competitor.

I hope you've enjoyed these 9 Ways to Amazon-Proof Your Business. I encourage you to visit the links I have for you at the end of each chapter.

Once you've squeezed everything you can out of it, set this book aside for a while. Pick it up and read through it again at a later date. In my business journey I've found that there's more value in being reminded of what I need to do, as opposed to just learning it one time. I 've needed many reminders before the most important lessons have "sunk in." If you're the same, come back to this book again and again for gentle reminders.

Now that we're done, let me know what you think about the book: brianjpombo.com/amazonbookreview

If this book brought up other questions, reach out to me at: BrianJPombo.com

Good luck and remember that "Fortune favors the bold." Be bold as you set forth to stand out from your competition!

About the Author

BRIAN J. POMBO is an author, podcaster, and business strategist who helps successful business owners break through obstacles & rekindle their passions. Brian has been helping companies overcome marketing, infrastructure, and management problems since 2007. He has worked with global brands that include Craftsman, Shell, Jaguar, and Sony. He lives in Grants Pass, Oregon with his wife Kate and their three children.

You can connect with me on:

https://brianjpombo.com

CPSIA information can be obtained
at www.ICGtesting.com
Printed in the USA
BVHW052007070821
613766BV00002B/30

9 781649 214010